Seasons of the Deciduous Forest Biome

Written by
Shirley Duke

Rourke
Educational Media

rourkeeducationalmedia.com

Scan for Related Titles
and Teacher Resources

www.rourkeeducationalmedia.com

PHOTO CREDITS: Cover: Olha Afanasieva; Title page © Becky Sheridan; page 4 - map © Christian Lopetz, leaf © Carlos Caetano. notebook © PixelEmbargo; page 5 - © Chiyacat; page 6 - © Elenamiv, sticky note © Neyro; page 7 - © Cynthia Kidwell; page 8 - © akarapong; page 8 - inset photo © Yellowj; page 9 © outdoorsman; page 10 © Inga Nielsen; page 11 © petersemler-photography; page 12/13 © Mark R; page 14 © Dmytro Pylypenko; page 15 © Volodymyr Burdiak; page 15 inset photo © tomatto; page 16 Tony Campbell; page 17 © Eric Gevaert; page 18 © Wessel du Plooy; page 19 © Vsha; page 20 © spirit of america; page 21 © Hurst Photo

Edited by Jill Sherman

Cover design by Renee Brady
Interior design by Tara Raymo

Library of Congress PCN Data

Seasons of the Deciduous Forest Biome / Shirley Duke
(Biomes)
ISBN 978-1-62169-898-2 (hard cover)
ISBN 978-1-62169-793-0 (soft cover)
ISBN 978-1-62717-005-5 (e-Book)
Library of Congress Control Number: 2013936814

Also Available as:
ROURKE'S
e-Books

Rourke Educational Media
Printed in the United States of America,
North Mankato, Minnesota

Rourke
Educational Media

rourkeeducationalmedia.com
customerservice@rourkeeducationalmedia.com • PO Box 643328 Vero Beach, Florida 32964

Table of Contents

All Four Seasons

Deciduous forests change through the year. The broad leaves on the trees in deciduous forests show the passing seasons. Maple, oak, hickory, and beech trees fill deciduous forests.

Deciduous Forests have:

✓ Four distinct seasons
✓ Rich soil
✓ Tall canopy of trees
✓ Lower levels of shrubs
✓ Diverse wildlife

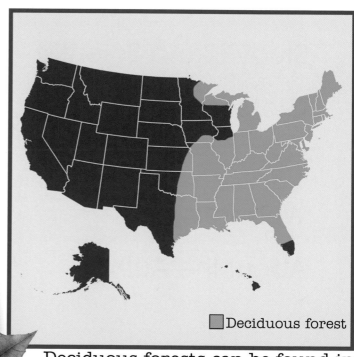

☐ Deciduous forest

Deciduous forests can be found in the eastern half of North America.

5

In fall, green leaves turn bright red, brown, and yellow. Then the leaves float to the ground. They land in piles under the bare branches. The leaves **decay** and make the soil rich.

In fall, cool air and short days tell trees to stop growing. Trees then stop sending water to the leaves. Green colors fade. The bright fall colors show.

Deciduous trees offer shelter and food to animals. Insects, **salamanders**, and spiders find food in the fallen leaves.

Skunk

Fallen tree trunks make homes and food for many kinds of life.

The bare trees rest all winter.

Some evergreen trees also grow in deciduous forests.

8

In winter, some animals leave for warmer places. Others sleep through the snow and ice. Foxes and owls stay all winter. They hunt creatures under the snow.

Great-horned owl

Owls and foxes use their hearing to find mice and chipmunks under the snow.

The tree leaves grow back in spring. The leaves' broad shape catches sunlight and makes food for the trees.

Shrubs grow under the canopy. Wildflowers and berries rise between shrubs. **Mosses** and ferns carpet the ground.

Wildflowers grow and bloom in the sunlight shining through the canopy.

Summer is a time of growth.

With more hours of daylight, spring and summer months provide a long growing season for the deciduous forest.

Young animals grow larger and stronger.

White-tailed deer

Life in the Trees and Leaves

Squirrels, skunks, and raccoons live among the trees. Rabbits hide and chipmunks gather seeds.

European red squirrel

Forest hawk

Woodpecker

Jays, woodpeckers, and hawks live and hunt in the forests.

Many animals have coloring that blends in with the ground. The colors help them hide.

White-tailed deer

Foxes, bobcats, and mountain lions hunt deer and small animals. Bears eat berries and fish, but will eat anything else they can find.

Red fox

Future of Deciduous Forests

People use and enjoy deciduous forests.

They hike, camp, and fish in forests.

They cut trees for wood. They clear land and farm the rich soil.

More people live in the deciduous forest biome than any other biome.

But cutting down forests removes animal homes. Air **pollution** harms the leaves. Mining and fires change forests for a long time.

Help preserve the forests for the future.

You Can Help
Protect Forests:

✓ Use fewer paper products made from trees.
✓ Recycle paper.
✓ Pick up your trash from your forest visits.
✓ Plant a tree by your home.
✓ Reduce air pollution by walking instead of driving.

People can preserve deciduous forests by making them into national parks to protect them.

Study Like a Scientist
Leaves Losing Water

1. Pick a green leaf.

2. Lay it on a plate.

3. Look at it each day.

4. What happens?

The leaf loses all its water like trees do in winter. With no more water, the leaf turns brown and dies.

Glossary

decay (di-KAY): to rot or break down into smaller parts

deciduous forests (di-SIJ-oo-uhs FOR-ists): a group of trees that drops their leaves every fall

mosses (MAWS-uhz): a fuzzy, green plant that grows on damp ground, walls, and tree trunks

pollution (puh-LOO-shuhn): harmful matter in air or water that can cause problems with life

salamanders (SAL-uh-man-durz): small, soft-skinned animals with four legs that are in the amphibian family

shrubs (SHRUHBZ): small bushes with woody stems

Index

Websites

www.nhptv.org/natureworks/nwep8c.htm

kids.nceas.ucsb.edu/biomes/temperateforest.html

inchinapinch.com/hab_pgs/terres/d_forest/td_forest.htm

About the Author

Shirley Duke has written many books about science. She lives in Texas and New Mexico and loves the different seasons in each place. She recently hiked a section of the Appalachian Trail that went through a deciduous forest. She loved the beautiful moss and fungus growing on the rocks, tree trunks, and forest floor.

Meet The Author!
www.meetREMauthors.com

24